Franz Kafka and Prague

TEXTS: Prof. PhDr. KAREL MARTÍNEK DrSc.

PHOTOGRAPHS: MIROSLAV HUCEK

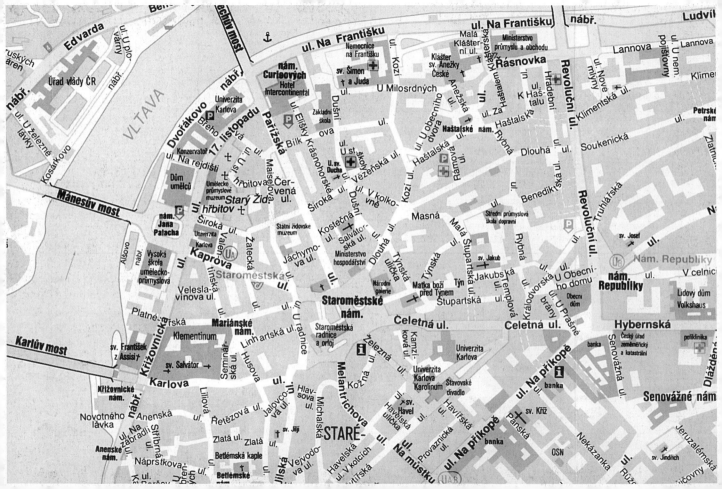

FRANZ KAFKA
AND PRAGUE

Around modern-day Prague
in the footsteps of Franz Kafka

"I always have the feeling that in some ways I understand Kafka better than others do. Not on account of possessing a better and deeper intellectual awareness of his work, but rather owing to a very personal and existential appreciation of it, which stems from a certain - if I may be permitted to say it - spiritual affinity..."

Václav Havel: Letters to Olga

ISBN 80-85822-30-X

This quotation from a letter written from prison by Václav Havel to his wife Olga is included here not just as an incidental tribute to the President of the Czech Republic but as further evidence of an undeniable fact: that any in-depth study of Kafka's literary and philosophical work has to stem from a purely personal response. Of course our academic knowledge of that work also plays an important role, as do our direct experiences of those places connected with Kafka's life in Prague, where - excepting a few brief absences - he spent all of his childhood, adolescence and adulthood.

The Czech poet Pavel Eisner was not far from the truth when he wrote that "Only through Prague can we come to a true understanding of Kafka..." But not, of course, through today's Prague, whose appearance has seen a great many alterations, some less fortunate than others. Around the turn of the century the city was a meeting point for cultural influences from Paris, Berlin and imperial Vienna, and the old Jewish spirit too thrived here in an enclosed community, of which - owing to large-scale destruction work carried out in the ghetto around 1906 - all that remains is a handful of synagogues, the key buildings of the old Jewish Quarter. This unique blend of Czech, German, Austrian and French influences formed a rich and inimitable local culture in which Prague's German literature - with the names of Max Brod, Egon Erwin Kisch, Franz Werfel and others - was a dominant element.

Prague, Kafka's birthplace, does more than simply provide the setting for his prose, a backdrop against which he depicts with increasing intensity the plight of the human being as he is crushed by bizarre circumstances and forced by a process of alienation into another, thoroughly inward-looking world, in a subjective testimony of experience and confession that was to become a feature of much literature of the 20th century.

As is known, Kafka was born on 3rd July 1883 on U radnice (originally Mikulášská ulice), in house number 5. His father, thanks to his enterprising nature and a good deal of hard work, had by this time become a successful wholesale merchant in haberdashery. His authoritative character is known to have had a negative effect on the whole family and in particular to have destroyed his son's self-confidence. From June 1889 the family lived in house number 2 on the Old Town Square (Staroměstské náměstí), where three daughters were born - Gabriela (Elli), Valerie (Valli) and Otylie (Ottla). To the north of the Old Town Square was Prague's ancient Jewish Quarter, and in the area now occupied by the elegant Pařížská třída ('Parisian Avenue') life bustled on in little houses and shops occupied by dozens of families with countless children. In 1905 a rather insensitive 'slum clearance' project was carried out, following which all that remained of the former Jewish ghetto was its town hall, six synagogues and the old cemetery with its tomb of the legendary Rabbi Löw (Jehuda Löw ben Bezalel), revered Cabbala scholar and - according to legend - creator of the Golem. This destruction meant more than just architectural change, for the liquidation of the ghetto brought with it the ascendancy of Czech influence over German in the Old Town of Prague. The previously isolated Jewish community was now exposed to the atmosphere of the times, in which the Czechs were attempting to assert their national interests within the Austro-Hungarian Empire. Their endless dances, exhibitions and processions must have seemed quite repulsive to those accustomed to life in an environment free of national borders, and all these Slavic celebrations of course had a minimum impact on the young Kafka, a pupil at the German Boys' School (Masná ulice 6) and then at the German Grammar School in the Kinský Palace on the Old Town Square, constantly engaged in conflicts with his domineering father. The Czechs were living life to the full, caught up in nationalist fervour and rightfully longing for those favours enjoyed by their neighbours in the Austro-Hungarian Empire.

The most important event of Kafka's years as a Jewish grammar school student was the bar mitzvah ceremony that took place on 13th June 1896 in the former Jewish synagogue (at Elišky Krásnohorské 33), confirming his attainment of adulthood and religious erudition. In the autumn of the same year the Kafka family moved to the house 'At the Three Kings' (dům U tří králů), at Celetná 602.

Photographs from this period show Kafka as a large-eyed, tight-lipped child with a questioning gaze, whether as a little boy of five on a toy pony or as a grammar-school student with crew cut and protruding ears. The similarities here, particularly given the time span of approximately ten years between the two pictures, confirm that Kafka was always a

pensive individual eager for knowledge and clearly marked by the despotism of his father. His deep eyes and tightly shut lips are perhaps suggestive of his future destiny as a world-famous writer.

After leaving school in 1901 Kafka took a holiday at the spas and visited the island of Helgoland. He began his studies of German language and literature and attended a law course at the German University in Prague, in what is now the court building on Ovocný trh. There he befriended Hugo Bergmann, a leading personality among the Jewish academics of Prague, who took him onto the editorial staff of the magazine Selbstwehr.

While staying with his uncle's uncle, the country doctor Siegfried Löwy, in Třešť in 1902, Kafka met a number of interesting personalities including Max Brod and Oskar Baum, and on his return to Prague he became a loyal member of the Café Louvre literary circle (at Národní třída 12). In his later years as university student he attained the position of art and literature officer of the association of lecturers and readers, where it was his task to keep up to date with newly published books and magazine studies. These were moments of the greatest importance in the broadening of his spiritual horizons, the bridging-over of his spiritual isolation and the formation of friendly ties with quite a number of interesting people, primarily with the writers and artists of the future.

Kafka's days as a law student came to an end, and in 1906 he entered ordinary working life, first in the office of his uncle Richard Löwy as articled clerk, probationer and clerk, then at the civil and criminal court, then with an Italian insurance company (Assicurazioni Generali, Wenceslas Square 19) and finally at the Workers' Personal-Accident Insurance Company for the Czech Kingdom (Na poříčí 7).

His career reached its high point in 1922 when he was promoted to secretary-in-chief. Such work proved to be a great source of literary inspiration for Kafka, for it was in these various offices that he became acquainted with the unwillingness of authorities to meet the fundamental needs of the individual and with the plight of the human being surrounded by insensitive characters, inhuman mechanisms, crushing bureaucracy - all fundamental themes in his future writings.

Some relief from office life was provided by Kafka's meetings with the intellectual company that was gathered around Max Brod, the Prague Literary Group (including Willy Haas, Rudolf Fuchs, Otto Pick and Franz Werfel), which held its meetings and discussions in various Prague cafés including the Café Savoy (Vězeňská 11), the Café Arco (Hybernská 16) and the Café Continental (Na příkopě 17). Among other, similar cultural groups in Prague at the time was the philosophical circle surrounding Otto and Bertha Fanta, which met at the House at the Unicorn (dům U jednorožce), number 18 on the Old Town Square.

In the Prague of the first decade of the century Czech national and social issues were coming to a head, while the Jewish intelligensia continued in its condemnation of any racial and nationalist prejudice. It was in this atmosphere that Kafka became acquainted with Czech literature and began to understand Czech culture, although of course independently of the nationalist jingoism of the period. His encounter with Slavic culture inevitably drew his attention to the east, leading him back to the tales of the Hasidic Jews, and to this was added his interest in an Eastern European Jewish theatre group which, under the direction of Jizchak Löwy, performed old Jewish stories in Yiddish in Prague.

So, on the one hand there was Kafka's job in the Workers' Personal-Accident Insurance Company, where he worked from 1908 until 1922, and on the other the artistic world of literature and theatre, a paradoxical combination explicable only in terms of the generally contradictory nature of this sensitive individual, who constantly sought refuge in his own private world of visions, fantasies and boundless imagination. German philosophical circles, literary groups and Jewish theatre society were the elements that shaped the destiny of this future writer trapped in the bureaucratic environment of the insurance company. For Kafka and his literary work the routine events of everyday life took on a special meaning, for he observed them, snatched them up and with his extraordinary way of perceiving things transformed the most banal happenings into something quite out of the ordinary. For whole nights he stayed awake "writing like fury", even though he was fully aware of just what this might cost him. But the possibility of death, madness, losing family and friends did not frighten him. He rather accepted it as the inevitable price of his devotion to his work, which itself posed questions touching the very essence of human existence.

With the exception of his various literary friendships and other literary stimuli elsewhere in Prague, and of his business trips to Liberec and Frýdlant and visits to Zürich and Lugano, Kafka's life went on primarily within a limited area of the city, that in the immediate vicinity of the Old Town Square and the streets Na příkopě and Na poříčí. Rather more important to Kafka than his excursions farther afield were his brief escapes from an environment in which he was finding it ever more difficult to breathe - and not only on account of the ill health that was already approaching. One unfortunate event in this period was a clash with his father, who was intending to put Franz in charge of the family's asbestos products factory, a situation which intensified his thoughts of escape by suicide.

A radical change came in the way of his relationship with Felicie Bauer, one that was to be accompanied by numerous separations and reconciliations and a great deal of agonizing contemplation. On 20th September 1912 Kafka's correspondence with Felicie began, and during that night he wrote his story The Verdict, in which genuine personal confession takes on a literary form. On one hand he yearns for friendship and a more interesting way of life - and on the other he cannot break his lifetime's habits as a loner permanently marked by his father's commandeering. Sadly, his body was already beginning to "betray" him at this time, the signs of tuberculosis becoming increasingly evident, and so it became necessary for him to seek treatment at the sanatorium in Junborg and to take on work as a gardener in Trója, a green suburb to the north of the centre of Prague.

In the following period Kafka gave a public reading of The Verdict, drafted seven chapters of his unfinished novel

America and began work on The Trial. The latter, set in Prague, corresponds most accurately to his spiritual disposition at this time. His first publisher now appeared: Kurt Wolf, whom Kafka met in Leipzig.

Kafka considered marriage with Felicie Bauer and at the end of July 1913 carefully compared arguments for and against a wedding. His 'escape' from the situation consisted in an attempt at suicide by jumping from a window. His first literary successes - including publication and the 1915 Kleist Award - date from this period.

With the beginning of the First World War Kafka was obliged to vacate his flat (Mikulášská ulice 36) for his sister Elli and her two children. His wanderings then took him to rented rooms in Bílkova ulice (in what is now house number 16, not far from the Intercontinental Hotel), Dlouhá třída (in the House at the Golden Pike, today number 16) and Zlatá ulička (Golden Lane, number 22) at Prague Castle. Sometimes he was disturbed by the neighbours, at other times he objected to the noise from the street. In March 1917 he finally settled at the foot of Petřín Hill, at Na tržišti 15, which now houses the United States embassy. In this apartment he worked on The Trial and a number of short stories. It is not by chance that the Castle, the cathedral of St Vitus, the Hunger Wall on Petřín and other Prague sights feature in his works of this period. The next tragic moment in Kafka's life came in August 1917, when he began coughing up blood - a sign that tuberculosis was advancing. By this time he and Felicie had become engaged for the second time, but another parting necessitated by a trip to Budapest proved to be the last, for a definitive break-up followed. The sad end to this love affair was, however, overshadowed by greater worries in the form of Kafka's unrelenting bad health, which was further complicated in the autumn of the following year by a severe bout of influenza. His reduced lung capacity was unable to bear the fevers, and Kafka's supremely healthy intellect was let down by an increasingly sick body.

Kafka spent time in boarding houses, in Siřem and in Želízy, where he met Julie Wohryzek, the daughter of a warden of a Prague synagogue. In her presence his long-time thoughts of the possibility of taking on liberating physical work in an agricultural commune finally began to take concrete shape, and Julie and Franz, "sensibly getting engaged" beforehand, planned their departure for Palestine. Whilst in Želízy Kafka also wrote his famous Letter to my Father, a generalized account of all that painfully inflicted the psyche of a sensitive individual.

While Kafka was undergoing treatment in Merano the Czech writer and journalist Milena Jesenská was working on a translation of one of his stories, and with her he entered into a regular correspondence that gradually developed into a serious relationship, so that in the autumn of 1920 he broke off his engagement with Julie Wohryzek. The affair with Milena gave Kafka a certain new hope. His extensive correspondence with her reveals much about his inner feelings at that time; these are the vacillations of a broken spirit in the closing phases of its life. The diaries he left with her have come to be an essential source of information on Kafka both as a person and as a philosopher on the threshold of the 1920s, a period marked by great changes on the world map. Empires were disintegrating, and raging war was bringing out the most brutal in humankind. And so all the more strongly cried out the voice of a wounded soul unable to come to terms either with a life of dull monotony or with one characterized by the destructive influences that were deforming mankind ...

In the spring of 1921 Kafka fell ill once again, suffering high fevers and inflammation of the intestine. One year later came nervous collapse, and in desperate conditions he completed The Castle. Kafka saw emigration to Palestine as the way out of his extreme - and worsening - nervous state, and so devoted himself to the study of Hebrew. The last woman with whom he had a relationship was Dora Dymant, a nurse at a holiday camp for Jewish children from Berlin at a summer resort on the Baltic coast.

Kafka's condition continued to worsen. During short periods of relative stability he devoted himself to the study of Jewish culture and history, as if anticipating the forthcoming suffering of the Jews at the hands of the Nazis. Following a stay at the German summer resort of Müritz, studies of Judaism at the university and a brief holiday in Dobřichovice, near Prague, Kafka visited a sanatorium near Vienna, where he died on 3rd June 1924.

However, Kafka had not left Prague for good; he was laid to rest here in the new Jewish cemetery, part of the Olšany cemetery complex. Prague is linked inextricably with his life and work: the city was his home and his inspiration, both a refuge and a source of danger for him. Here he was born within the sphere of influence of the former Jewish ghetto and went to school and university. Here, working as a legal clerk, he searched for an identity, the identity of an individual as well as of a German Jewish intellectual. This is where most of his key literary works - novels, stories and correspondence - were produced. Here he would walk across Charles Bridge and up to the Castle with its magnificent cathedral, pass below lofty church spires, and wander among the little shops and stands of the gradually disappearing ghetto to the north of the Old Town Square, near which he lived and worked. From the romantic island of Kampa he looked out over the Vltava as it flowed through Prague. This author of bitter, painful tales was - according to Milena Jesenská - shy, nervous, gentle and kind. A case of the conscience dictating to the pen, for Kafka was unable to remain silent in the face of the indifference of those surrounding him. He did not feel safe in this humbling and humiliating world.

Then there is the question of the extent to which Prague has accepted Franz Kafka. The advocates of Socialist Realism in the last half-century or so did not greet his writings with a great deal of sympathy. Stalinist ideology was unable to accept Kafka's philosophical concepts, as analogies with the political regime were made all too clear in his work, and analogy revealed more than enough. Kafka's references to man surrounded by misunderstanding, man wounded and humiliated by insensitivity, man as supreme being regardless of all his faults and doubts... all this was reason enough for playing down Kafka's contribution to the development of world literature.

The recently established Franz Kafka centre and exhibition on the Old Town Square in Prague may, then, be considered as part repayment of an old debt. A great deal of information, including numerous editions of his works, illustrated books and guidebooks, is now available, making it possible for us to walk in the footsteps of Kafka through modern Prague. It is still not so easy, however, to see beyond the veil of today's mass culture and mass media into the past, and Prague as Kafka knew it - a unique melting-pot of Czech, Jewish, German and Austrian cultural values - is irretrievable.

Finally, although those totalitarian barriers to knowledge of Kafka's work throughout Central and Eastern Europe have now fallen, of course the indifference and superficiality of those who turn a blind eye to the dangers of terrorism, nuclear accidents, war in the former Yugoslavia and so on, unfortunately did not disappear along with them. And so, in conclusion, a few thoughts from Kafka's Aphorisms...

"There are just two primary human sins from which all others stem: impatience and indifference. Impatience got Adam and Eve expelled from Paradise, and indifference prevented their being let in again..."

"Only the spiritual world really exists. What we call the world of the senses is purely an evil in the spiritual world, and what we call evil is just the necessity of a moment in the eternity of our development."

"Essentially we are expelled from Paradise for ever. That expulsion is unretractable, and life in this world is inescapable. However, the whole, eternal process (or rather the eternal repetition of the process) still offers us the possibility of dwelling permanently in Paradise, whether we are conscious of that fact here or not."

"As regards Earth, man is both free and bound, because he is fastened to Earth by a chain that is long enough to allow him access to all its parts but not long enough for anything to be able to snatch him from within its bounds. And as regards Heaven he is equally free and bound, for he is fastened to it by a second chain similarly calculated. He may go anywhere, and he is aware of it. But should he wish to go to Earth the Heavenly collar will choke him, and should he wish to go to Heaven the Earthly collar will do the same. And yet he refuses to blame this on his Earthly mistake..."

Kafka's Life in Facts

1883: Kafka is born on 3rd July at Mikulášská 9 (now U radnice 5) in the Old Town.

1889-1896: He lives with his parents and three sisters at Old Town Square 2.

1889-1893: He attends the boys' school at Masná ulice 16.

1893-1901: He is a pupil at the Old Town's German Grammar School in the Kinský Palace, Old Town Square 12.

1896-1907: The Kafka family lives at the House at the Three Kings (U tří králů), Celetná 3.

1901-1906: Franz is a student of law at the German University in Prague, Ovocný trh 5.

1906: He is employed in the offices of his uncle Dr Richard Löwy at Old Town Square 16.

1906-1907: He gains experience of work in the civil and criminal courts.

1907: Kafka begins work in an Italian insurance company at Wenceslas Square 19.

1908-1922: He is employed at the Workers' Personal-Accident Insurance Company for the Czech Kingdom at Na poříčí 7, first as a casual worker, then as clerk, as vice-secretary, as secretary and finally as secretary-in-chief.

1910: He attends meetings of the philosophical circle of Otto and Bertha Fanta in the House at the Unicorn, Old Town Square 22, and of the Prague Literary Circle in various places including the Café Savoy (Vězeňská 11), Café Arco (Hybernská 16) and Café Continental (Na příkopě 17).

1910: The first dated entry in Kafka's diary is from 16th December of this year. (The last is from 12th June 1923).

1912: The Verdict is completed on 20th September. Chapters of the unfinished novel America follow.

1913: The Kafka family moves to Oppelt's House at Old Town Square 5. Kafka himself moves first to Bílkova ulice 10 and later into the flat of his sister Elli on Nerudova (today Polská 48), where he writes most of The Trial between September 1914 and February 1915.

1915: Kafka lives in rented accommodation in the House at the Golden Pike, Dlouhá třída 16.

1916-1917: From November 1916 to August 1917 he rents a house in Golden Lane at Prague Castle (today U Daliborky 2).

1917:	He moves to Na tržišti (present-day location of the United States Embassy), returning to h parents' apartment at Old Town Square 5 following a worsening in his condition.
1918-1920:	He seeks treatment in various locations - Siřem, Želízy, Merano (northern Italy), Tatranské (Slovakia) ...
1921-1922:	... Prague, Špindlerův Mlýn and Planá nad Lužnicí.
1923:	He rests in Dobřichovice, on the Baltic coast and in Berlin. He longs to return to life, tak Hebrew and attending university lectures on Judaism.
1924:	Kafka is seriously ill. He returns from Berlin to Prague, and then goes to Austria for sana treatment. He dies in Kierling on 3rd June 1924. He is buried in the new Jewish cemet Strašnice in Prague.

Sources

I. Herrmann, J. Teige, Z. Winter: Pražské ghetto [The Prague Ghetto] (Prague, 1902)
Juden in Prag [The Jews in Prague] (Prague, 1927)
J. Janáček: Malé dějiny Prahy [A Brief History of Prague] (Prague, 1977)
Kafka [exhibition catalogue] (Prague, 1991)
Pražské synagogy [Prague's Synagogues] (Prague, 1986)
R. Pytlík: Pražské kuriozity [Prague Oddities] (Žďár nad Sázavou, 1993)
C. Rybár: Židovská Praha [Jewish Prague] (Prague, 1991)
C. Rybár: Franz Kafka a Praha [Franz Kafka and Prague] (Prague, 1991)
H. Volavková: Zmizelé Pražské ghetto [The Vanished Prague Ghetto] (Prague, 1961)

FRANZ KAFKA'S PRAGUE

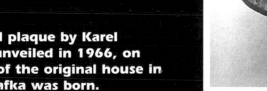

ZDE SE 3.7.1883 NARODIL FRANZ KAFKA

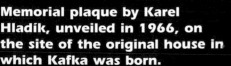

Memorial plaque by Karel Hladík, unveiled in 1966, on the site of the original house in which Kafka was born.

Building that now stands on the site of the former House at the Tower (dům U věže), in which Kafka was born. Of the original house, which was pulled down in 1897 during the demolition of the Jewish Quarter, only the doorway remains, now a floor higher than in its original position. The exhibition Franz Kafka is located here.

The expanding Kafka family moved into the medieval House at the Minute (dům U minuty), at Old Town Square 2, alongside the Old Town Hall. During the family's residence here, from June 1889 to 1896, Kafka's sisters were born and young Franz himself first went to school. At that time the house was not quite so impressive in appearance, its rich sgraffito decoration not being restored until some time later.

View of the church of Our Lady before the Týn from Štupartská street. Not far from here, in the house at Celetná 3, Kafka's family spent a further eleven years. On the ground floor Franz's father had his shop, above which the family occupied quite a large apartment. This was where Kafka's originally Czech father made the definitive transformation into prosperous German businessman. He attended the Pinkas synagogue and sent his children to German schools.

Fun and games in the streets of the ancient ghetto came to an end for the young Franz when he began to attend the German boys' school at Masná street.

Before finally settling
in the House at the Minute,
the Kafka family had lived
in a number of locations:
on Ve Smečkách,
on Wenceslas Square,
on Dušní, on Mikulášská
(now Pařížská) and at Celetná 2
(the house on the right).

The window from which Franz Kafka, from his flat, was able to observe the services held at the church of Our Lady before the Týn.

Hermann Kafka had his haberdasher's shop in the Kinský Palace, on the corner nearest the recently restored medieval House at the Stone Bell (dům U kamenného zvonu). Now the family was able to afford a larger apartment and no longer had to move so frequently from one residence to another.

The magnificent Kinský Palace housed the German Grammar School that Franz Kafka attended from September 1893 until July 1901. The Kafka family's flat and shop were also situated here - everything under one roof! In the immediate vicinity of the Old Town Square Kafka lived, attended school and grammar school, wrote and walked each day to his job in the insurance offices. And so he was justified in his statement that "...the whole of my life is bound up in this small circle...".

The building of the Carolinum, which in Kafka's day housed the German University in Prague. He studied here from the autumn of 1901, officially as a student of law, although he also attended lectures on German literature and art history. On the right of the picture is the side entrance to the Estates Theatre (Stavovské divadlo), renowned for its performances of Mozart's operas.

The impressive Clam-Gallas Palace, and in the background the Clementinum, originally the centre of the Jesuit order and later home to the German University and extensive libraries.

View of Hradčany from the iron Svatopluk Čech Bridge, which was actually being constructed while the Kafka family was living at the end of Pařížská (then Mikulášská). The green hills that rise above the municipal swimming pool appear in The Verdict.

Hradčany seen from the pillars of the Svatopluk Čech Bridge, around which the Academy of Applied Arts, the Museum of Applied Arts and later the building of the philosophical faculty of the Charles University also emerged. The square here is named after Jan Palach, a student who burned himself to death in 1969 in protest against the Soviet invasion and the suppression of the Prague Spring. Beyond the museum lies the Old Jewish Cemetery and a labyrinth of streets with monuments surviving from the former Jewish ghetto.

Franz Kafka graduated as Doctor of Law on the 18th June 1906, having also completed a compulsory year's work at the civil and criminal court on Ovocný trh. In October 1907 he began work at Assicurazioni Generali, an Italian insurance company that occupied an impressive house on Wenceslas Square, on the corner with Jindřišská.

After less than one year of working there, Kafka left the Italian insurance firm and entered into employment at the Workers' Personal-Accident Insurance Company for the Czech Kingdom, at Na poříčí 7. He began in 1908 as a casual worker and after two years was promoted to clerk. Three years later he became vice-secretary. In 1920 he became secretary, and just before his retirement (for health reasons) in 1922 he was made secretary-in-chief. He worked here, then, for a total of fourteen years and became thoroughly acquainted with the mechanisms of administrative practice, with all its bureaucratic conventions... . But there was free time too, time to meet friends, visit the theatre and devote himself to his writing.

Before the First World War literary creativity blossomed in Prague, thanks to a unique synthesis of Czech, German, Austrian and Jewish cultures. Kafka was introduced to literary society by Max Brod, and the two of them, together with Felix Weltsch and Oskar Baum, took excursions into the area around Prague, led passionate debates and came to form an essential element in Prague's literary-café world. As, for example, at the Café Continental, situated in the Kolowrat Palace at Na příkopě 17.

Franz Kafka and his friends also visited the Café Savoy at Vězeňská ulice 11. Clearly defined literary and discussion groups developed on the Prague cultural scene, frequenting the city's many cafés. Of special importance to Kafka was the Prager Kreis, Prague's German literary group, among whose members were Max Brod, Franz Werfel, Rudolf Fuchs and Willy Haas.

The building on the corner of Skořepka was another centre for discussion groups. Franz Kafka wrote and published the impressions he gained on his wanderings through Prague and also kept detailed diaries. Some of the diaries were later destroyed by Dora Dymant in accordance with Kafka's own wishes, while others disappeared thanks to confiscations made by the Gestapo.

Another of the many retreats of Kafka's friends and literary companions - the Café Arco at Hybernská ulice 16, not far from the present-day Masaryk Station. Max Brod coined the term "Arconauts" for visitors to this café, a term to which the German intellectuals and poets did not object.

Looking through the Powder Tower (Prašná brána) into Celetná, with the Týn church in the background. This was the view Kafka had each day as he walked to the Workers' Personal-Accident Insurance Company on Na poříčí.

View from Kafka's room in Oppelt's House on the corner of Mikulášská (now Pařížská) and the Old Town Square. Kafka had a fine view of the statue of St Nicholas in the Church wall and of the elaborate Prague coat of arms.

Kafka's retreat during the autumn of 1920 - again, Oppelt's House. Here he continued work on the novel The Castle.

When in 1914 Kafka had to vacate the family apartment at Pařížská 36 for his sister Elli and her children, he found rooms in Bílkova ulice - not far from where the Intercontinental Hotel stands today - and later at Dlouhá třída 16, in the House at the Golden Pike (dům U zlaté štiky).

From 1910 German literary groups met in the House at the Unicorn (at Old Town Square 22), which housed a pharmacy.

For a short period Kafka occupied a flat at Bilkova ulice 10. The Spanish Synagogue can be seen in the background.

The building at Národní (formerly Ferdinandova) třída 12 that housed the Café Louvre. Around 1902 the café Union, opposite here, was the venue for meetings of Brentano and his circle. As a student at the university Kafka was attracted to the Jewish academic society Bar Kochba and to those involved with the magazine Selbstwehr. This might have been where Kafka began to discover great literature, the spiritual heritage of European civilization, one that was being deformed by absurdities and inhumanities.

Kafka's longing for peace and quiet and the chance to concentrate fully on his work led him to this little house, number 22 on Golden Lane (Zlatá ulička), which was rented by his youngest sister Ottla. Here he wrote The Country Doctor. But discomfort and a lack of space soon forced him to move on.

Kafka moved down from his little house in the grounds of the Castle to the foot of Petřín, taking accommodation at Na tržišti 15, which now houses the United States embassy. Here he wrote The Building of the Great Wall of China, connected with the Hunger Wall that runs up Petřín Hill. Unfortunately his relative happiness here was cut short by the onset of sickness. Kafka began coughing up blood - tuberculosis had arrived.

The new Jewish cemetery in Olšany, Prague, took over from the old cemetery in Žižkov, where burials had taken place up until 1890. In the new cemetery visitors will find the six-sided tomb (number 21 14 21) where Franz Kafka rests together with his parents. Hermann Kafka died in 1931, Julie Kafka three years later. A tablet at the foot of the tomb remembers his three sisters, who perished in 1942 and 1943 at the hands of the Nazis. The cemetery contains a number of notable tombstones from the workshop of the famed sculptor Jan Štursa. Czech writer Ota Pavel, poet Jiří Orten and painter Max Horb are among the other well known personalities to have been buried here.

JEWISH PRAGUE

On Pařížská třída, not far from the 'Old-New' (Staronová) Synagogue, stands a statue of Moses by František Bílek, of whose work Kafka was a great admirer.

The Old-New Synagogue (Staronová synagoga) on Červená ulice, and the High Synagogue (Vysoká synagoga). The first is one of the oldest Gothic buildings in Prague, and the second dates from the Renaissance. The Old-New Synagogue is austere and strictly functional, as was the custom with buildings of this kind from the second half of the 13th century. It is thought that a building workshop involved also in work at the convent of St Agnes contributed to the construction of this synagogue between 1270 and 1280. The prayer hall is impressive in its dimensions and has not only served as a venue for religious ceremonies, for in the Middle Ages this was where the legal matters of the Jewish town were discussed. Seats in the hall were bought and passed down families from one generation to the next, and seat number one is said to have been that of the legendary Rabbi Löw. This large stone structure has been witness to numerous ghetto fires and tragic pogroms.

By the almemor with its Torah stand, a faded red flag bears the message "Lord, our Judge, the whole world is filled with His glory. In the year 1357 the Emperor Charles IV bestowed upon the Jews of Prague the privilege of this, their own standard...". The text continues, explaining that the flag was repaired during the reign of Ferdinand and praising the majesty of Archduke Leopold... It also bears the Star of David and, in its centre, the characteristic pointed Jewish hat, without which Jews were not allowed to leave the ghetto.

The Jewish Town Hall on Maislova ulice. The precise date of its origin is not known, although it might already have been standing by 1567 and it is first mentioned in documents of 1577. Following a fire, reconstruction in the Baroque style threw it into contrast with the austere facade of the High Synagogue. Its tower has a gallery with an elaborate Baroque railing and a star at its top. On the main facade is a Jewish clock with Hebrew numerals and with hands that move in 'reverse', while the clock on the tower itself has Roman numerals. The building still serves the administrative purposes of the Jewish community and houses an excellent kosher restaurant. This is also a venue for musical performances and other cultural events.

Detail of grille, with the motifs of six-pointed star and pointed hat.

The Renaissance High Synagogue originally formed one structure with the neighbouring Town Hall. Dating from around 1568, it served the function of prayer room for the town hall, being intended for use by council representatives and for meetings of the rabbinic court. It belongs to a group of buildings that was saved from destruction by Mordecai Maisel, one-time mayor of the Jewish town. The interior of the High Synagogue has something of a secular feel about it, being somewhat reminiscent of the halls at Prague Castle. Gradually this synagogue became separated from the Town Hall, its east portal was altered and a staircase was added inside.

The Old Jewish Cemetery, burial place and monument, a unique memorial of world importance. In the background is the Klaus Synagogue, one of the oldest buildings in the Jewish Quarter. It dates back to 1564 and was formed from several smaller, independent buildings referred to in documents as 'klausy' (= hermitages), which gave it its name. Following a fire in the ghetto in 1689 the original group of smaller buildings was replaced with a single, larger structure that came to serve various functions, including that of retreat of the Jewish burial association.

The Pinkas Synagogue, on Široká ulice. Archaeological digs in the underground part of the synagogue have brought to light an old well and ritual baths dating from the 13th century or early 14th. On the site there also once stood one of the oldest synagogues ever, first mentioned in 1492. The complex story of the ownership of the Pinkas Synagogue relates it to the House at the Coats of Arms (dům U erbů), where the name of Pinkas also appears. The prayer hall belonged to the Horovic family, and Aaron Meshulam Horovic, great-nephew of the founder Rabbi Pinkas, made alterations to the structure in 1535. Pronounced Renaissance elements brought about by later reconstruction work have not been preserved. The fairly inconspicuous doorway of this synagogue conceals a beautiful interior with reticulated vaulting characteristic of Jagellonian-period Gothic architecture.

In 1960, in the extensive interior of the Pinkas Synagogue, built to house a congregation of 500, there was created a monument to the 77 297 Jewish victims of the Nazi Occupation; the names of those who were tortured and executed or who perished in concentration camps are written across the synagogue's walls. The names of Prague Jews are given in alphabetical order, together with birth and deportation details. The names of Slovak victims are not included, owing to the fact that Slovakia was an independent state during the Second World War. This is one of the longest epitaphs in the world.

The Maisel Synagogue, on Maislova ulice. The land for the building of this synagogue was bought by Mordechai Maisel, prosperous mayor of the Jewish Quarter, in 1590, and its prayer hall was consecrated in 1592. The original building was a triple-naved structure with twenty columns, and following a fire it was reconstructed on a more modest scale, its original length being reduced by a third. An organ similar to that in the Spanish Synagogue was installed here in accordance with the needs of the new Jewish rite. Today the synagogue houses a unique exhibition of Silver from the Synagogues of Bohemia, a collection of objects used in religious ceremonies by 153 Jewish communities and including Torah-scroll adornments, extensions and pointers as well as silver goblets and candelabras, tin wedding plates, brass Hanukkah candlesticks, table lamps and many other items.

The Spanish Synagogue, in Vězeňská ulice, was built some time in the 11th century or the 12th as part of a settlement of Jews of eastern (Byzantine) origin. On arrival here these eastern Jews had formed their own ghetto, which remained quite independent of that centred on the Old-New Synagogue. The two Jewish districts were physically separated by the Catholic church of the Holy Ghost, part of a Benedictine convent. The Jewish scholars in this unique Prague district also had a command of Czech and other Slavonic languages, as is demonstrated by the margin notes they jotted into their Hebrew religious books. The reformation of the Jewish rite called for the installation of an organ, which was entrusted to the care of the Czech composer František Škroup, author of the song Kde domov můj (Where is my homeland?) for Tyl's play Fidlovačka (= the name of an old festival formerly held in Prague each spring). This song was to

become the Czech national anthem. The fact that a non-Jewish Czech composer worked in the synagogue is an indication of the tolerance and cultural acceptance that were very much features of this particular Jewish community. The imposing interior of the Spanish Synagogue is the result of reconstruction work carried out between 1882 and 1893. The synagogue is striking in its square plan with large cuppola and ornamental decoration and in its colourful windows in the Spanish style adopted from Alhambra.

An inscription over the gallery of the old ceremonial hall reads "Holy Society performing good deeds".

The Old Jewish Cemetery on U starého hřbitova - 'at the old cemetery'. This replaced an older cemetery that was located in the area of present-day Vladislavova ulice and Spálená ulice, in the New Town, where burials took place from 1270 to 1478. Some Gothic tombstones were transferred here to the Jewish Quarter from the original cemetery. Space limitations in the ghetto meant that the cemetery's only chance of expansion was vertically, so that the graves here - around 12,000 of them - occur in twelve layers.

Gothic tombstones brought to the Jewish Quarter from the old cemetery between Vladislavova ulice and Spálená ulice. The oldest legible inscriptions reveal the earliest of the stones to be from either 1346 or 1351.

A modern copy of the Old Jewish Cemetery's oldest tombstone, whose original is kept in the State Jewish Museum. It is from the grave of Rabbi Abigdor Kar, author of an elegy on the devastation of the ghetto in 1389, and gives the date of the Rabbi's death as 25th April 1439, making it arguably the oldest stone here - excepting, of course, those brought here from the older burial ground and incorporated into the wall of this cemetery.

Although the Jewish faith did not favour the representation of the human form, human figures do actually appear here, and more frequently than in other cemeteries. One tombstone bears stylized figures of Adam and Eve in the Paradise Garden, in the tradition of naive folk art. Legend has it that this is the resting place of two young newlyweds claimed by the Angel of Death on their wedding day.

Symbols on the graves represent allegiance to families, social groups and trades, and often to the priesthood in particular. The Cohen family, who in Biblical times belonged to the priesthood, are represented on their stones by the symbol of two blessing hands. This is the tombstone of Katz Fanta from 1628.

Another priestly tribe dating from Biblical times is that of Levi (the Levites), whose symbol is the ritual vessel used for pouring water over the hands of the faithful, a symbol of the priesthood as well as of purification.

The oldest tombstones are usually the simplest - sandstone tablets either straight or semicircular at the top and decorated only with script. The texts, however, are in relief and so do add sculptural depth to the stones, the words sometimes also spilling over beyond the chiselled-out frames.

The Renaissance tomb of Mordechai Maisel (1528-1601), one-time mayor of the Jewish Quarter. He was also a financier and patron whose achievements include the initiation of the building of the Maisel Synagogue. In the Renaissance sandstone was replaced by white or pink Slivenec marble in the building of tombstones, and wealthy citizens would often have four-walled tombs built, something along the lines of sarcophagi.

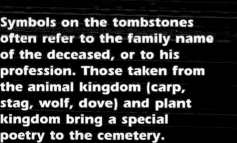

Symbols on the tombstones often refer to the family name of the deceased, or to his profession. Those taken from the animal kingdom (carp, stag, wolf, dove) and plant kingdom bring a special poetry to the cemetery.

Headstone with lion, from the ornate Renaissance tombstone of Hendela, wife of Jacob Bashevis, a leading financier of Italian origin who attained vast wealth through coin production. While his two wives and five children are buried here in the Old Jewish Cemetery, Jacob himself ran away from the ghetto before a trial and died in Mladá Boleslav in 1634.

The tombstone of the most renowned figure of the Jewish Quarter, Jehuda Liva ben Becalel, or Rabbi Löw, also known by the name of MAHARAL, an acronym formed from the Hebrew words meaning 'our teacher, our master'. The life of Rabbi Löw (1520-1609), scholar and founder of the rabbinic school here in the Prague ghetto, is enshrouded in legends, including that of the Golem, a clay figure he brought to life with a Cabbalistic spell. The tombstone of the Rabbi's grandson Samuel, whose wish it was to be laid to rest alongside his

grandfather, was squeezed into the little remaining space next to the Rabbi's grave, and rumour has it that Rabbi Löw's stone moved over of its own accord to make room for that of his grandson. The tomb is linked with secret powers and is attributed with the ability to grant wishes - in the manner of the Wailing Wall in Jerusalem - so that visitors to the cemetery often leave their private wishes, written on little pieces of paper, tucked into the cracks in the tomb. It is also dotted with little stones, in accordance with an ancient tradition whereby nomadic Jews used stones to protect the bodies of their dead from beasts of prey. The fact that Rabbi Löw also excelled as a speaker and Talmud scholar is less widely known than the mysteries and legends that surround him. An expert on the subject of Neoplatonic philosophy, he became Chief Rabbi in the Czech Kingdom and worked also in Mikulov and Poznaň.

THE ATMOSPHERE OF HISTORIC PRAGUE

Coat of arms of the city of Prague at the entrance to the church of St Nicholas on the Old Town Square, a Baroque treatment of medieval motifs - knights' helms with crests, fortifications, a portcullis - framed by lions, symbol of the Czech lands.

The side entrance to the church of Our Lady before the Týn, by the Old Town Square. The Kafka family lived in various apartments in the vicinity of this church, and Franz's father had a haberdasher's shop in a corner of the neighbouring Kinský Palace.

Alleyways, tight corners and house signs, all that survives of the Middle Ages in the little streets around the Týn church, evoke the atmosphere of the extinct Jewish ghetto.

Neo-Gothic tower on the Smetana Embankment, now missing its original statue of the Austrian emperor, which was removed in 1918 when the independent Czechoslovak Republic was declared.

One of the highest points in Prague - the summit of Petřín with its observation tower, a copy in miniature of the Eiffel Tower in Paris. On the left there is one of the statues on the Charles Bridge, the oldest preserved bridge in Prague, founded by Charles IV, king and emperor, in 1357.

Looking towards the Strahov Monastery from Charles Bridge, with its rows of mainly Baroque statues. This structure replaced the original (11th-century) Judith Bridge and has played an important role in the history of the Czech lands since the reign of Charles IV. Franz Kafka wrote a poem about the bridge in 1902:

Crossing dark bridges,
People pass saints
With little faint lights.
Traversing grey skies, Clouds
Pass churches
With dusky spires.
Resting on a wall,
A figure gazes into
The evening water,
Hands on ancient stones.

The atmosphere of an evening on Charles Bridge. In the background are the Lesser Town bridge tower and the cuppola and tower of the church of St Nicholas in the Lesser Town (which, incidentally, is not connected in any way with the church of the same name on the Old Town Square).

Gothic gargoyles with the faces of devils at the cathedral of St Vitus in the grounds of Prague Castle. One of the chapters of The Trial is set here.

The main nave of the cathedral of St Vitus – the oldest part of the cathedral, where the tombs of princes and church dignitaries are to be found. Among them is the tomb of St John of Nepomuk with its silver lamps. Up on the gallery are busts of Czech kings and the cathedral's architects.

In Kafka's *The Trial*, K's route to the execution ground takes him to deserted spots whose atmosphere is evoked by the present-day appearance of the area that surrounds the city walls by the Strahov monastery, on Pohořelec.

"... they stood on the edge of a free and open space that was unpeopled ..."

Vast, bare walls and empty windows lit up by sudden rays of sunlight. Another passage from The Trial comes to mind:

"... the shutters of one window flew open and the light burst its way in ..."

One of the entrances to the stone wall. It appears to conceal something secret and mysterious beyond. In the words of Kafka's character K. in The Trial, "I shall go no further ..."

"A little stone pit," in the words of Kafka's novel *The Trial*, "desolate and deserted, not far from a rather townish house. Where is the judge he never set eyes upon? Where is the high court he never came before?" Here ends the life's pilgrimage of K.

KAFKA'S LIFE IN BRIEF

The family. Franz's father, Hermann Kafka (1852-1931), successful businessman who worked his way up from small shopholder to wholesale merchant. The fact that his shop was located on the Old Town Square indicates that he had definitively left the conservative and overpopulated Jewish ghetto for Prague's German-speaking society. His domineering nature is widely recognized as having marked the young Franz for life. This photograph shows a well-off, self-assured businessman. Kafka's mother Julie (1855-1934) was unable to prove a stronger parental influence than her dominant husband. She gave birth to six children, of whom two died - Georg/Jiří (1885-1886) and Heinrich/Jindřich (1887-1888). Besides Franz, three girls survived - Gabriela (1889-1941), Valerie (1890-1942) and Otýlie (1892-1943). All three sisters, along with their husbands and children, were later to perish in the Nazi concentration camps. It was in Otýlie's flat that Kafka wrote a number of stories in late 1916 and early 1917. Kafka's relationship with the head of the family is outlined in his Letter to my Father of 1919: "In your presence I lost all self-confidence, trading it for an endless guilty conscience...".

THE KAFKA FAMILY TREE

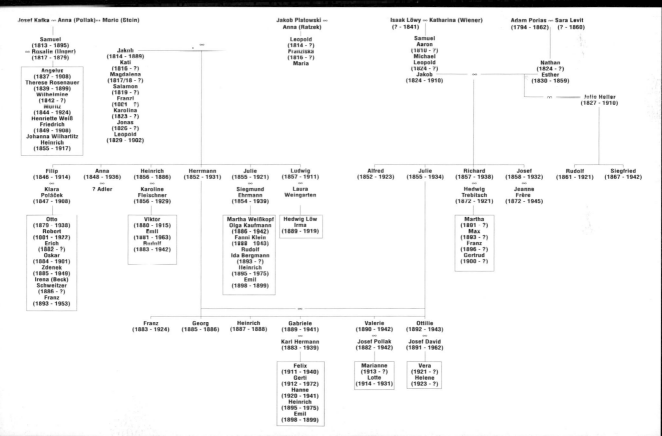

1852 – 1931

1855 – 1934

1883 – 1924

1889 – 1941

1890 – 1942

1892 – 1943

Franz Kafka in 1888, aged five. He appears unusually serious for his age, individual in his looks. On seeing this photograph Max Brod commented on Kafka's "large, questioning eyes and tightly closed, obstinate mouth."

A photograph from 1893 showing Franz, aged ten, with his sisters Otýlie (or Elli), in the middle, and Valerie (Valli), on the left. The age difference between Franz and the two girls was (respectively) nine and seven years. Correspondence of the period reveals that Franz provided them with a sensitive upbringing. He was gentle, tactful, considerate

A photograph from Fuchs' studio, from the earlier years of Franz's studies at the grammar school, between 1893 and 1901. A lanky adolescent with a striking appearance.

Franz as a mature grammar school student, around 1901 or later.

A photograph from the second half of the 1890s, and probably after 1896. This is the type of picture that would typically have been mounted on the school-leavers' picture board at graduation time.

Until 1901 Franz Kafka studied at the eight-year State German Grammar School, which was housed in a Baroque palace on the Old Town Square. His father's haberdasher's shop was located in the same building. The facade of the Kinský Palace has not changed a great deal since then, although the shops have disappeared. This is again a well dressed young man with individual features and a dreamy look.

In the autumn of 1901, having left school, Kafka enrolled at the German University in Prague, then located in the Carolinum. He studied law but also attended lectures on art and literary history and German studies. He was not greatly satisfied with his studies here and considered transferring to the university in Munich, but finally he decided (as he writes in letters of the time) that Prague had him too firmly in her clutches...

Kafka's strict parents forced him to complete his studies, which also involved gaining a year's compulsory experience of work at the civil and criminal court on Ovocný trh. Here he learned about the workings of the court and about bureaucratic convention. Kafka eventually graduated as a Doctor of Law on 18th June 1906. His face does not seem to express a great deal of satisfaction here, rather terror of the now inevitable move into the world beyond...

Between 1911 and 1912 Kafka was very much occupied with Jewish history and the question of a collective Jewish mentality, through - among other groups - a Jewish theatrical company from Lvov. He began to learn Hebrew at this time, and devoted time to the study of Hasidic legends, which were to have a great deal of influence on his writings.

Kafka at the time when he had begun work on his now world-famous novel The Trial, perhaps in August 1914. At this time he was still moving from one apartment to the next in search of peace and quiet for concentration on his writing: from Dlouhá třída to Zlatá ulička (Golden Lane) to the Old Town Square. His impaired self-confidence, the result of his father's strictness, weakened his ability to write regularly and systematically. But he sought refuge in the company of his sisters and acquaintances, and winning the Kleist Prize in 1915 was a great moral support to him.

Tranquil times with the family - Franz with his youngest sister in front of Oppelt's House in 1915. One of the more peaceful moments in the otherwise turbulent period of the First World War and Kafka's complicated relations with Felicie Bauer, with whom he went through several breakups and reconciliations. All part of the torturous drama of this highly sensitive individual not quite cut out for the harsh world around him - which made tranquil moments like this one all the more precious.

Kafka met Felicie Bauer through the writer Max Brod. Their love affair was a breath of inspiration for Kafka and left its mark on all the work he produced throughout 1912, although correspondence of the period reveals his inner worries concerning his "betraying body", his advancing sickness. His first engagement to Felicie was called off and a second was followed by a definitive break-up. Here his idol appears a good deal more mature and experienced than does Kafka himself.

On a visit to his beloved sister Otýlie, who had taken over the running of the family estate in Siřem, near Podbořany. His first visit here was in 1917, the second a year later, when in his sickness he spent four months here. Following the final split with Felicie and his first attack of blood-coughing he enjoyed a period of recuperation here. Otýlie, his favourite sister, tried to be of comfort to him in his unenviable situation.

According to the Franz Kafka exhibition in Prague this photograph shows the writer at the beginning of the First World War, although other sources date the picture to the year 1919.

An interesting picture usually dated to Kafka's stay in Matliare in 1921. The First World War is over, and the influence of American Paris has reached Prague - shorter jackets, centre partings, and of course the indispensable bow-tie on elastic. Kafka's expression in this picture seems to suggest that his illness has not yet surfaced.

Kafka on the Old Town Square, place of his birth and upbringing, probably at the time when he had begun writing The Castle - in 1920-21. He is in clothes fashionable at the time, and has the appearance rather of a student than of a renowned literary figure.

Hluboce zarmouceni podáváme zprávu že náš syn

JUDr. František Kafka,

zemřel dne 3. června t. r. v sanatoriu Kierling u Vídně, jsa stár 41 roků. Pohřben bude ve středu, dne 11. června t. r. o ¾4 hod. odpol. na israel. hřbitově ve Strašnicích.

V PRAZE, dne 10. června 1924.

Heřman a Julie Kafkovi,

jménem veškerého příbuzenstva.

Kondolenční návštěvy se s díky odmítají.

In tiefstem Schmerz geben wir bekannt, daß unser Sohn

JUDr. Franz Kafka

am 3. Juni im Sanatorium Kierling bei Wien, 41 Jahre alt, gestorben ist. Das Begräbnis findet am Mittwoch, den 11. Juni um ¾4 Uhr auf dem jüdischen Friedhof in Straschnitz statt.

PRAG, am 10. Juni 1924.

Hermann und **Julie Kafka,**
Eltern,
im Namen der trauernden Hinterbliebenen.

Von Kondolenzbesuchen bitten wir abzusehen.

One of the last photographs of Kafka, taken in Berlin in late 1923 or early 1924. Following his return to Prague he visited a sanatorium near Vienna, where he died on the 3rd June 1924. Here is face is marked by pain and suffering.

Franz Kafka's signature. A trained, flowing and energetic hand. Graphologists might well argue that this is not the signature of a tortured genius and doubt-ridden natural intellectual.

Czech and German versions of the announcement of Franz Kafka's death, signed by his parents. Following Franz's death the family refused all visits of condolence. On 19th June Hans Demetz, director of the Prague Municipal Theatres, organized a remembrance ceremony at the Kleine Bühne ('Little Stage') on Senovážné náměstí. A speech was given by Max Brod, who, as executor of the will, contradicted Kafka's wishes by refusing to burn his writings.

One of Kafka's little drawings in the
modern Cubist spirit - evidence of
his knowledge of world art and its
tendencies, and of his ability to
handle space and maintain human
expression in artistic miniature.
Kafka attended lectures on art and
displayed a degree of artistic talent.

Franz Kafka and Prague

published by freytag & berndt, Praha
first edition, 1998
photographs: Miroslav Hucek
texts: prof. PhDr. Karel Martínek, DrSc.
translation: Sarah Peters-Gráfová
typesetting: Ing. Milan Gattringer